Helping Children See Jesus

ISBN: 978-1-933206-29-5

THE WORD OF GOD
Old Testament Volume 16
Joshua Part 1

Author: Arlene S. Piepgrass
Illustrator: Vernon Henkel
Typesetting and Layout: Morgan Melton, Patricia Pope

© 2018 Bible Visuals International
PO Box 153, Akron, PA 17501-0153
Phone: (717) 859-1131
www.biblevisuals.org

All rights reserved. No part of this publication may be reproduced, stored in a retrieval system or transmitted in any form by any means, electronic, mechanical, photocopy, recording or otherwise, without the prior permission of the publisher, except as provided by USA copyright law.

RELATED ITEMS

To access related items (such as activities, memory verse posters and translated texts) please visit our web store at shop.biblevisuals.org and enter 2015 in the search box on the page.

FREE TEXT DOWNLOAD

To access a FREE printable copy of the teaching text (PDF format) in English or other available languages, enter S2015DL in the search box. Add the item to your cart, and use coupon code XTACSV17 at checkout. Once your order is processed you will receive an email with a link to the free download.

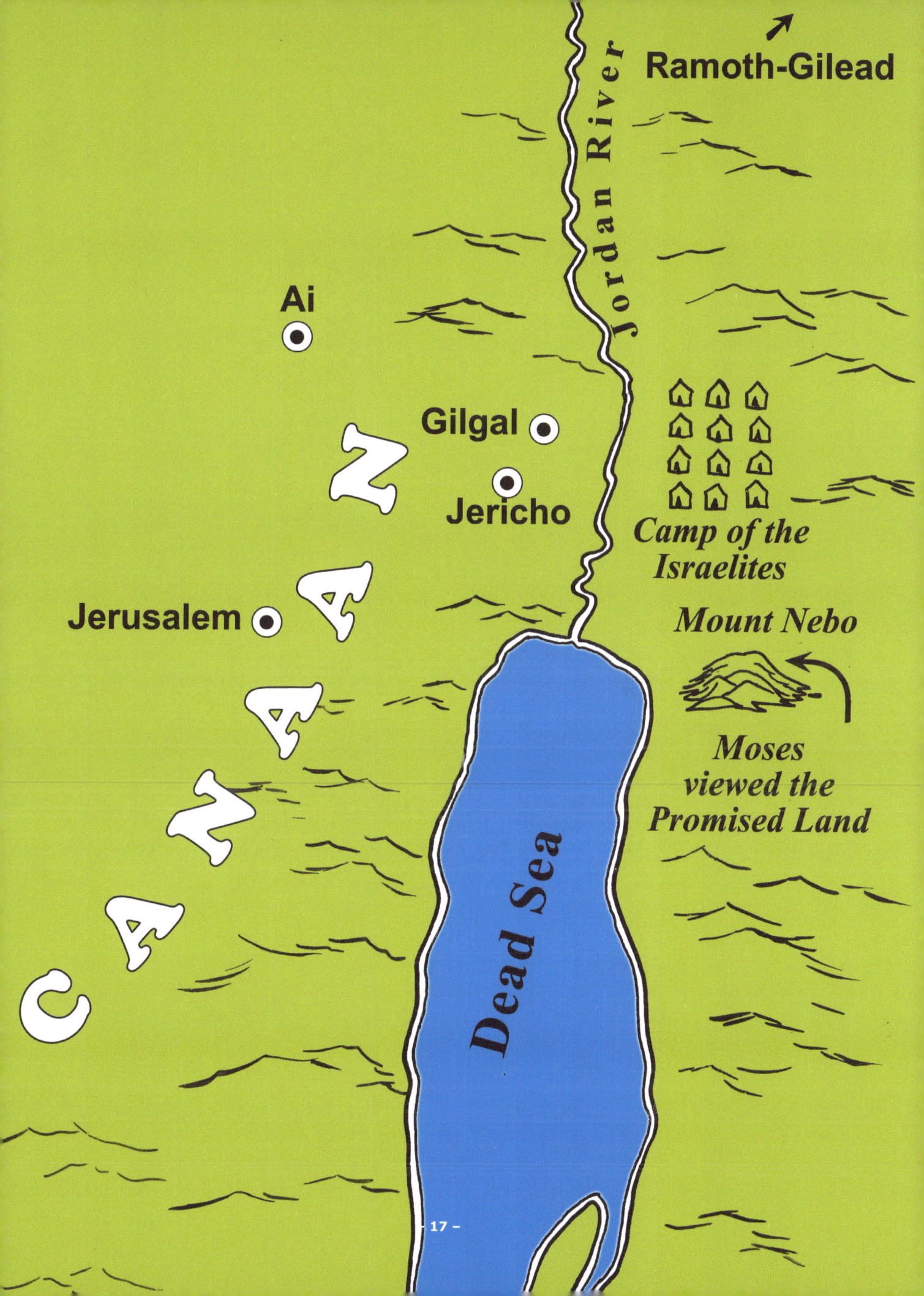

This book of the law shall not depart out of thy mouth; but thou shalt meditate therein day and night, that thou mayest observe to do according to all that is written therein: for then thou shalt make thy way prosperous, and then thou shalt have good success.

Joshua 1:8

Lesson 1
KNOWING GOD'S WORD

Scripture to be studied: Joshua 1; verses cited in lesson

The *aim* of the lesson: To show the importance of meditating upon (studying and thinking about) the written Word of God.

What your students should *know*: That a good leader must know and obey God's Word.

What your students should *feel*: A strong desire to study the Word of God and live by it.

What your students should *do*: Read God's Word every day; pray that the Holy Spirit will help them obey it.

Lesson outline (for the teacher's and students' notebooks):

1. Joshua served God under Moses (Exodus 17:5-13; 24:13; 32:1-35; Numbers 13:1–14:45).
2. Joshua listened to God's Word (Joshua 1:1-9).
3. Joshua believed God's promises (Joshua 1:1-9).
4. Joshua followed God's commands (Joshua 1:10-18).

Remember! No one can become a good leader who has not first learned to be a good follower!

The verse to be memorized:

This book of the law shall not depart out of thy mouth; but thou shalt meditate therein day and night, that thou mayest observe to do according to all that is written therein: for then thou shalt make thy way prosperous and then thou shalt have good success. (Joshua 1:8)

NOTE TO THE TEACHER

Joshua continues the history of the people of Israel. It marks the end of their wanderings in the wilderness and the beginning of their new lives in Canaan. God had promised Moses He would lead them to the land of Canaan—the same land He had promised to Abraham more than 400 years before. (See Exodus 3:8; Genesis 12:1-3; 15:13-21.)

The book of Joshua provides historical accounts of: (1) the Israelites' conquest of Canaan under the leadership of Joshua; and (2) the division of the land among the 12 tribes.

There are many spiritual lessons in Joshua showing those who believe in Christ how to live lives of Christian victory. Ask the Holy Spirit to apply these truths to your own life before you teach them to your students.

Our first lesson emphasizes the importance of God's *written* Word. Impress upon your students the need for reading and studying God's Word regularly and prayerfully. Only then can they *know*, *believe*, and *obey* what He says.

THE LESSON

Do you belong to a family? Do you have rules in your home? How do the children in a family know the family rules? (Their parents tell them.)

When we trust in the Lord Jesus Christ for salvation from sin, we are born into the family of God. (See John 1:12.) God has rules for His family. He also gives His children many wonderful promises. He has written His rules and promises in His Word, the Bible. And He wants us to read His Word, believe it and obey it.

Today we are beginning the study of Joshua, another Old Testament book. Forty years before the time of this book, Moses led the Israelites out of Egypt. (See Exodus.) While the people of Israel were in the wilderness, God gave them His law so they would know how they should live. God also taught them how they should worship Him. (See Leviticus.)

The Israelites could have entered the land God promised them quite quickly. But because they disobeyed Him, they were punished. They wandered in the wilderness outside their promised land for 40 years. (See Numbers.) At the end of that time, Moses died and God buried him–no one knows where. (See Deuteronomy 34:5-6.)

Before Moses died, God commanded him to turn over his leadership and authority to Joshua. God had chosen Joshua to replace Moses. (See Numbers 27:15-23; Deuteronomy 34:9.)

Who was Joshua? Would he be able to lead over 2,000,000 people? Would he be able to defeat their enemies in Canaan?

1. JOSHUA SERVED GOD UNDER MOSES
Exodus 17:8-13; 24:13; 32:1-35; Numbers 13:1–14:45

(*Teacher:* If you have not recently taught the lessons of Genesis through Deuteronomy, you may want to make two lessons out of this one. By so doing you can review the events of Joshua's life in more detail than is given here.)

Joshua was born in Egypt. He grew up there and was one of the Israelite slaves who worked in the brick kilns (Exodus 33:11). He saw the men being beaten day after day by the Egyptian taskmasters. He may have been beaten many times himself.

Joshua was in the crowd which sang God's praises the day God led them through the Red Sea on dry ground. Joshua saw the Egyptian soldiers drown in that same Red Sea.

When the people of Israel escaped from Egypt, this former SLAVE (Joshua) had to become a SOLDIER. Soon after the Israelites began their journey through the wilderness, the army of Amalek came to fight against them.

Show Illustration #1

Moses commanded Joshua, "Choose men and lead them to fight against the army of Amalek."

Joshua was immediately ready to obey. While Moses prayed on the hilltop, Joshua and his men defeated Amalek's army.

Joshua was a SERVANT. He patiently waited on the mountain 40 days and 40 nights while Moses was receiving from God the instructions for building the tabernacle. (See Exodus 24:13; 32:17.)

Coming down from the mountain, Moses and Joshua heard the people in the camp singing and shouting. They were bowing down to the golden calf they had made–acting as if they were still in Egypt. Joshua realized how angry Moses was when he saw the people's terrible sin. And Joshua knew how Moses prayed to God for his people and for himself. Having served faithfully under Moses, Joshua was ready to learn from the example of this great leader.

Joshua was also a SCOUT. When the Israelites reached the border of the Promised Land, they asked Moses to send some men into Canaan to see what it was like. Joshua was one of the 12 spies who spent 40 days searching the land trying to learn all about it.

When they returned to the camp, Joshua was ready to go forward and conquer the land as God had commanded them. He and Caleb) told the people, "It is an exceedingly good land. Let us enter Canaan immediately. The Lord is stronger than the people in the land. And He is with us. Do not be afraid!"

But, sad to say, ten of the spies discouraged the people. They told them, "We are as small as grasshoppers compared to the giants in Canaan!"

Joshua heard God's severe judgment: "None of you who are 20 years and older will enter the land except Joshua and Caleb who believed Me. The rest of you will die in this wilderness!" (Numbers 14:29).

Exactly as God said, those people did die. Their children grew. And Joshua became their LEADER. He had been chosen and prepared by God.

2. JOSHUA LISTENED TO GOD'S WORD
Joshua 1:1-9

Show Illustration #2

Listen to God's command to Joshua. "Moses my servant is dead. Now cross this Jordan River–you, and all these people. Go into the land which I promised to give them."

Suppose you had been Joshua. How do you think you would have felt? (*Fear, inadequacy, uncertainty.* Let students discuss.)

Joshua must have been afraid because God said to him, "Do not be afraid or discouraged, Joshua, because I am with you."

What would make Joshua afraid? (Encourage student response.)

God said, "Cross the Jordan River!" But how? The river banks were overflowing. (See Joshua 3:15.) There were more than 2,000,000 people with their animals to get across. They had no boats. This would be dangerous!

God said, "Go into the land!" But there were many huge, strong people dwelling in the land. They lived securely in cities surrounded by high walls.

For 40 years Joshua had heard the Israelites grumble. Over and over they had refused to obey God. Yes, Joshua had good reasons to be afraid. These people were rebellious.

But Joshua was ready to listen to God.

God said, "Joshua, do not be afraid. Do not be discouraged. Be strong and very courageous. You have My written Word. (Before Moses died, God had caused him to write down the first five books of the Bible. This was all that Joshua had at that time.) Talk about My Word, Joshua. Study it. Think about My

promises day and night. Obey all that is written in it. My Word will be your guide. Do all it commands. Obey Me, Joshua, and you will be successful!"

3. JOSHUA BELIEVED GOD'S PROMISES
Joshua 1:1-9

Show Illustration #3

As Joshua continued to listen, God gave him some wonderful promises.

1. The promise of God's purpose (Joshua 1:3, 6).

   "Joshua, I am now going to give you the whole land of Canaan just as I promised Abraham (Genesis 13:14-17) and Moses (Exodus 3:8; 23:27-33). Wherever you put your foot down, the land will be yours. I want you to divide it among the 12 Israelite families."

2. The promise of God's success (Joshua 1:5).

   God also promised, "None of the people in Canaan will be able to stand up against you. I will make them afraid of you. (See Deuteronomy 11:25.) You will be victorious! They will be defeated!"

3. The promise of God's presence (Joshua 1:5, 9).

   "Joshua, I will be with you all the way," God said. "I will never leave you. You can depend on Me."

What do you think Joshua should do with promises like these? (Let students discuss. Joshua should believe God means what He says. He should put his confidence in God, obey Him and trust Him completely.)

Suppose Joshua had answered: "Yes, God, those are wonderful promises You have given me. But I am not sure You will be able to keep Your Word. I am not sure You will be strong enough to conquer our enemies. I am glad You have given me Your Word to study. But being the leader of so many people keeps me busy. I am not sure I shall have much time to study and think about (meditate on) Your Word." What would you think of Joshua if he had answered this way? (Let students give opinions.)

Joshua did not say such things to God. He was ready to believe God's promises. But there are many people today who answer God this way. Maybe you are one of them. You might not say it with words. But your actions say it.

God wants us to meditate (study and think) upon His Word just as He commanded Joshua. (Read some of the following verses slowly and distinctly to your students. Emphasize the importance of studying God's Word daily, thus knowing His promises and His will. Psalm 1:1-3; 119:11, 15-16, 92-93, 97-99, 105, 130, 133, 165; John 15:4-14; Colossians 3:16.)

4. JOSHUA FOLLOWED GOD'S COMMANDS
Joshua 1:10-18

How do we know Joshua believed God? Because he immediately made plans to follow all God's commands. There was work to be done. Trusting God does not mean we sit back and do nothing. It means we work, knowing God will help us.

Show Illustration #4

Calling his leaders together, Joshua commanded, "Go through the camp and order the people to get ready to move. We are going to cross the Jordan River. We are going to take over the land God is giving us!"

The leaders answered, "Joshua, all that you command us, we will do. Wherever you send us, we will go. We shall listen to you just as we listened to Moses when he was our leader. We are praying that God will be with you as He was with Moses. Do not be afraid. Be strong and courageous!"

Joshua was ready to serve God with all his energy. He listened to God and believed God. Because he trusted God, he was not afraid of people.

And because Joshua studied God's Word and thought about it day and night, God was in control of all he did.

He obeyed the commands God had given.

He heeded the warnings of God.

He believed God's promises.

He learned to know and follow God.

Do God and His Word control your life?

Teacher's note: Encourage your students to mark in their Bibles when they read a command, a warning, a promise, or a prayer. Suggest that they list these in their notebooks so they will remember what they have read in God's Word.

Lesson 2
GOD'S WORD IS SURE

Scripture to be studied: Joshua 2:1-24; 6:22-25

The *aim* of the lesson: To show that God's Word is sure.

What your students should *know*: They can completely trust God's Word.

What your students should *feel*: Assurance that God keeps His promises.

What your students should *do*: Act in obedience to God's Word, believing He means what He says.

Lesson outline (for the teacher's and students' notebooks):

1. Rahab heard of God's power (Joshua 2:2-11).
2. Rahab reports fear in Jericho (Joshua 2:9-11).
3. Rahab acts in faith (Joshua 2:12-21).
4. Rahab rewarded for her trust (Joshua 6:22-25; Matthew 1:5; Hebrews 11:31; James 2:25).

The verse to be memorized:

This book of the law shall not depart out of thy mouth; but thou shalt meditate therein day and night, that thou mayest observe to do according to all that is written therein: for then thou shalt make thy way prosperous and then thou shalt have good success. (Joshua 1:8)

NOTE TO THE TEACHER

When the Israelites left Egypt, God promised He would cause their enemies to fear them. (See Exodus 15:14-16; 23:27.) As with all His promises, God kept this one perfectly. (See Deuteronomy 2:4; Numbers 22:3.)

Just before they moved into the land of Canaan, God showed Joshua that the people there were afraid of the Israelites. This confirmed again to Joshua that he could move ahead, confident of victory as he trusted God's promise.

Rahab did not know much about God. But she *believed* what she knew and *acted* upon it. Because she trusted God's Word and obeyed it, her life was saved.

Impress upon your students that they too can have this confidence in God's Word. **We have many** more promises than Joshua had. For he had only the first five Bible books: Genesis, Exodus, Leviticus, Numbers, Deuteronomy. God still **keeps all** His promises!

THE LESSON

What is a promise? (Let students define. A promise is a pledge to another to do or not to do something.) Do you always keep your promises? (Allow response.) Did anyone ever make a promise to you and not keep it?

There is One who never breaks His promises. Who is He? (The Lord.) God gave the Israelites promises and He kept those promises. God has given us even more written promises than they had. And He keeps every one of them. (See Titus 1:2.)

In our last lesson we learned that Joshua believed God's Word. How do we know this is true? (Joshua obeyed God's Word.) He acted upon it. As God commanded, he ordered all the people to get ready to march right across the Jordan River into Canaan.

Directly across the Jordan from the camp of the Israelites was Jericho, a big, wicked city. (Indicate on map.)

Joshua wondered, How strong is Jericho? How well-armed are the soldiers? Are the people there getting ready to fight us? To learn the answers to these questions, Joshua secretly sent two spies to Jericho. They crossed the Jordan River. The Bible does not tell us how. Maybe they swam across. We do know that the river was flooded at this time. (See Joshua 3:15.)

They walked in through the gates of Jericho, hoping no one would see them. They looked around and listened, trying to find out all they could for Joshua. They saw that the city was surrounded by big, thick double walls. The spies saw that the people worshiped idols. They saw the city had an army and a king. (See Joshua 6:2.) They saw that because the people were afraid, they kept the city gates heavily guarded.

Towards evening the spies looked for a place to spend the night. They knocked on the door of one of the houses built on top of the city wall. Rahab, the owner of the house, opened the door and invited them in. Even in that wicked city, Rahab had a bad reputation. She was not a good woman. She made her living by doing sinful things.

1. RAHAB HEARD OF GOD'S POWER
Joshua 2:2-11

Show Illustration #5

Rahab recognized that the two men were Israelites. She knew they were enemies. But she did not report them to the king's soldiers. Instead, she took them to the flat roof of her house. There she had piles of flax drying. (Flax is similar to hay.) "Lie down here and hide under these stalks of flax," she whispered. "No one will find you here."

At that moment someone else knocked at her door. This time there were detectives from the king of Jericho. "Rahab, we come with orders from the king," they announced sternly. "We know that two men entered your house. They are spies from the Israelites. They have come to learn about our city. The king commands that the men be delivered to him immediately. They are under arrest!"

Rahab answered, "Sirs, you are right. Two men did come into my house. I did not know where they came from nor why they came. But they did not stay. They left through the city gate. If you hurry, you might catch them."

Rahab had lied. But remember, she served idols. She had not been taught that lying is sin. God never excuses lying. It is one of the things He hates. (See Proverbs 6:17.) But Rahab did not at that time know God or His Word. Later, she was taught God's laws. Do you think she then confessed this sin and asked God's forgiveness?

The king's men rushed down the street, through the city gate and towards the Jordan River, hoping to capture the two spies.

All the while, the spies were safely hidden on the roof of Rahab's house. Why would Rahab plot against her own people like this? Why would she protect their enemies?

When the king's men were out of sight, Rahab went up to the roof to talk to the spies. "I know that your God is the God of Heaven and earth," she said. "Here in Jericho, we all worship idols which have no power to help us. Your God is powerful. We have heard how He opened the Red Sea for you to pass through on dry ground. We heard how He helped you to destroy King Og and King Sihon. (See Numbers 21:22-24, 33-35.) They were two of the strongest kings on the other side of the Jordan River. When we heard these things, we were terrified. Our men lost all their courage. We know that the Lord your God is God of Heaven and earth. We know that He is giving you our land. That is why I have protected you."

What Rahab had heard made her believe that the true and living God of the Israelites was greater than the false worthless gods worshiped in Jericho.

2. RAHAB REPORTS FEAR IN JERICHO
Joshua 2:9-11

Show Illustration #6

The two spies listened intently as Rahab continued talking.

"Everyone in Jericho is scared! No one has any courage to fight against you. They lock the city gates securely at night. They guard them carefully all day long. They are afraid you will destroy our city and kill all of us. Our people know they are not strong enough to defeat you. So they are afraid to fight you."

The two spies were astonished. This was exactly what God had promised. Forty years before (right after the Israelites crossed the Red Sea on dry ground) God had said that the people of Canaan would be afraid of them. So afraid, that they would not be able to resist them! (See Exodus 15:14-16.)

Later God had assured Moses, "When My people march into the land of Canaan, the Canaanites will be so scared they will flee before you!" (Exodus 23:27).

The spies must have said to themselves, "Thank You, Lord God. You are faithful! You keep Your promises! Your Word is truth!"

3. RAHAB ACTS IN FAITH
Joshua 2:12-21

"You know I have risked my life to protect you," Rahab told the two spies. "If the king hears that I hid you and lied to his men, I shall be killed."

The spies nodded their heads understandingly.

Rahab continued, "Will you do me a favor? When you march in and destroy Jericho, promise you will save my life and the lives of those in my family."

The spies promised, saying, "If you do not betray us, we shall protect you and your family from any harm."

"I will not betray you," Rahab promised. "Now, run to the mountains. Hide there three days. By then the men who are looking for you will have returned. Then you can hurry to your camp safely."

The spies understood. Then they gave instructions to Rahab. "There are two things you must do if you want to escape death:

1. Bring your mother, father and all your relatives into your house. Everyone in your house will be saved. If anyone leaves your house, we will not be able to protect them.
2. Put this scarlet rope in your window. It will mark your house from all the rest. When we see it, we will spare your house. Now remember! We will keep our promise if you do not tell anyone about our business. If you do, you will be killed along with everyone else in Jericho," the spies warned.

Show Illustration #7

Then Rahab–whose house was built on the city wall–helped the two men escape. They crawled out a window and she let them down to the ground by a scarlet rope.

Immediately Rahab fastened the scarlet rope in her window. Why did she do this? (Let students answer.) She trusted herself to God and His people. She believed they would do what they promised. The rope was scarlet. This is the color which reminds us of sacrifice through blood (Exodus 12:13; Leviticus 17:11) and of the precious blood of Christ. (See 1 Peter 1:18-19.)

What do you think Rahab did next? (Let students respond.) She doubtless went to her father's house as soon as it was safe. The Bible does not tell us what she said to them, but could it have been like this?

"Hurry, Mother and Father! Come to my house as quickly as you can! Tell my brothers and sisters and all our relatives to come, too. Jericho is going to be destroyed. Everyone is going to be killed. But if you come to my house, you will be safe!"

"How do you know this? When is it going to happen? Why will we be safer in your house than ours?" they asked fearfully.

Rahab told them all that had happened and cautioned them not to tell anyone else. Her family listened, believed her and went willingly to her house. There they stayed and waited.

The spies returned to the camp of Israel safely. Joshua was eager to hear their news. What do you think they told him? (Let one of the students read Joshua 2:24 slowly and distinctly. Or print the verse on paper ahead of time for all to read together.)

The Israelites did not need to fear. God had kept His Word! They could march into the land, certain of victory!

4. RAHAB REWARDED FOR HER TRUST
Joshua 6:22-25; Matthew 1:5; Hebrews 11:31; James 2:25

But that is not all the spies told Joshua. They told him also about Rahab. They told how she believed in the true and living God. They explained how she helped them and of the agreement they made with her.

During the next several days the Israelites prepared to cross the river. In our next lesson we shall learn what went on during that time.

Show Illustration #8

But right now we shall skip ahead to let you know what happened to Rahab. Jericho was destroyed. The people were killed–all except Rahab and her family. Joshua saw the scarlet rope in her window. The two spies rescued the whole family before the Israelites burned the city. Then Rahab and her family went to live with the Israelites. Later Rahab married one of the princes of Israel. (Compare Matthew 1:4-6 with Numbers 7:12.) And she became the great-great-grandmother of King David. Many generations later, the Lord Jesus Christ was born into this family. (Explain generation. We belong to one generation, our parents belonged to another; our grandparents to another, etc.)

Think of God's favor to Rahab. She was a wicked woman in an evil city. But she had faith in the Lord of Heaven. Because of her faith, she did what the Lord God told her to do. She was a traitor to her own people, but she was on God's side. To her, being loyal to God was more important than being loyal to her country. Because of her faith, she obeyed God's servants. And, in time, she became an ancestress of the Lord Jesus Christ, God's own Son. What an honor!

Did you know that you are in even greater danger than were the people of Jericho? God says you are in danger of being in a lake of fire separated from Him forever. (See Revelation 20:10-15.) This is God's judgment for everyone who refuses to place their trust in His Son, Jesus Christ. (See Luke 16:21-26; John 3:18, 36.)

But there is a way of escape. If you will receive the Lord Jesus as your Saviour from sin, you will one day be with Him forever in God's home–Heaven. (*Teacher:* read slowly and distinctly John 3:14-15; 1:12.) These are God's promises. (Read slowly John 10:27-29.)

Will you right now place all your trust in God's Son? He wants to give you His gift of eternal life. This is His promise recorded in His Word. And His Word is sure!

Lesson 3
GOD IS FAITHFUL TO HIS WORD

Scripture to be studied: Joshua 3, 4, 5; all verses cited in lesson

The *aim* of the lesson: To show that God is faithful to His Word. He cannot fail.

> **What your students should *know*:** That God sometimes tests the faith of His people by commanding what is humanly impossible.
>
> **What your students should *feel*:** Courage to trust God completely in every situation.
>
> **What your students should *do*:** Memorize God's promises and count on Him to keep His Word.

Lesson outline (for the teacher's and students' notebooks):
1. Preparations for crossing Jordan (Joshua 3:1-13).
2. Crossing the Jordan River (Joshua 3:14-17).
3. Two memorials set up (Joshua 4:1-18).
4. God's faithfulness to us (verses cited in lesson).

The verse to be memorized:

This book of the law shall not depart out of thy mouth; but thou shalt meditate therein day and night, that thou mayest observe to do according to all that is written therein: for then thou shalt make thy way prosperous and then thou shalt have good success. (Joshua 1:8)

NOTE TO THE TEACHER

We can trust God implicitly because He is faithful to His Word. His faithfulness is a pillar for our faith.

He is faithful in forgiving our sins. (See Proverbs 28:13; 1 John 1:9.) He is faithful in giving us grace and strength for all the circumstances He brings into our lives. (See 1 Corinthians 10:13; 15:57; 2 Corinthians 12:9; Philippians 4:13.) He will be faithful in giving us all He has promised for the future. (See 2 Timothy 2:11-13; 1 Corinthians 1:9; 1 Thessalonians 5:23-24.)

Such assurance should thrill your heart and strengthen your faith. Only as you trust God totally yourself, will you be able to challenge your students to do so. Encourage them to claim specific promises from the Bible and rely upon them.

Divide into two lessons if necessary. It will be helpful to review past incidents as suggested in the lesson.

THE LESSON

Did your father ever tell you to do something that seemed impossible for you to do? Were you afraid to try it? If he promised to help you, did that make any difference? Why? You knew you could trust him. (*Teacher:* Suggestions to stimulate answers: Did he ask you to jump from a high wall, promising to catch you? Or jump into deep water and swim, with his promise to grab you and help if you needed him? Encourage students to give personal incidents. Emphasize their trust in their father's promise and his faithfulness in keeping it.)

In our lesson today, God commanded Joshua md the Israelites to do something which seemed impossible. At the same time, He promised to help them do it.

1. PREPARATIONS FOR CROSSING JORDAN
Joshua 3:1-13

When the spies came back from Jericho, what encouragement did they bring to Joshua? (Review Joshua 2:24.)

The Israelites were camped right along the Jordan River. Early one morning the leaders went through the camp giving instructions. "Get ready to move. We are going to cross the river today. Take down your tents. Pack up your belongings. Herd your animals."

The people of Israel had moved many times. But this day there was much commotion. They were going to move into the land God had promised them.

But listen! The officers had another order for them. "When you see the priests carrying the Ark of God, follow it. Do not get too close. There must be a half-mile between you and the Ark, so all can see it."

What was the Ark of God? Let us recall some of the things we learned about it. (*Teacher:* Review with questions if you have taught Exodus and Numbers recently. If not, briefly explain.)

1. The Ark was a box made of wood, covered with gold.
2. The lid of the Ark was made of solid gold. It was called the mercy seat. On each end of the mercy seat was a solid gold cherub (a cherub is an angelic being). (See Exodus 25:10-22; 37:1-9.)

3. The Ark was kept in the Most Holy Place of the tabernacle. (See Exodus 26:31-35.)
4. Inside the Ark were:
    the tablets of stone with the ten commandments written on them
    a bowl of manna
    Aaron's rod that budded (See Exodus 16:32-34; Numbers 17:1-10; Deuteronomy 10:2, 5.)

    The glorious brightness of God's presence rested between the two cherubim on the mercy seat. (See Exodus 25:22; 40:34.)
5. Only the high priest ever saw the Ark itself. He was the only person who was allowed to enter the Most Holy Place and that only once a year.

While the people were preparing to move, the priests were covering every piece of furniture in the tabernacle. The furnishings would be carried on the shoulders of the Levites. The heavy curtains were loaded on wagons. (See Numbers 10:11-36; OT Volume 13 Lesson #3.) Finally everything was ready.

The people stood at the river's edge watching the water flow swiftly. All must have been wondering: How will we ever get across this river? It is flooded and the water is deep. We cannot wade across. We have no boats. How can we get the babies across? And all our animals?

Yes, it looked impossible. It was impossible for them. But nothing is impossible for God. He knew what He was going to do.

Joshua told the waiting people "Today God is going to do wonders among us. He is going to prove again that He is the living God. He is going before us as we cross the Jordan River. He will defeat all the enemies we shall meet in Canaan." What a wonderful promise!

Show Illustration #9

Then Joshua turned to the priests who were carrying the covered Ark. "Walk into the Jordan River!" he commanded. "As soon as your feet touch the water it will stop flowing. God has promised to hold back the river for us. Walk out to the middle. Stand there until everyone is across."

Joshua knew that he himself could not stop the Jordan River. But he was taking God at His word. God had promised that the waters would stand in a heap. Joshua was not afraid to expect the impossible. He knew that God never fails those who fully trust Him.

Joshua remembered what God had done with the Red Sea when His people were leaving Egypt 40 years before. (Review incident in Exodus 14:13-28.) Now he believed God would work another miracle.

2. CROSSING THE JORDAN RIVER
Joshua 3:14-17

The priests walked to the river, carrying the Ark on their shoulders. The people watched in hushed silence. The priests came closer and closer to the river. The water kept flowing as usual.

The priests touched the river with their feet. Instantly a miracle happened! The waters rolled back as if they were pushed by a mighty hand! Back, back, back they rolled until there was a path at least 16 miles wide! God had given His word and He had kept His promise. He pushed the waters back so far that they were completely out of sight! The priests walked to the middle of the river bed. There they stood holding the Ark.

Show Illustration #10

The people–more than 2,000,000 of them–started walking across. They led their animals–hundreds of thousands of them. All walked on dry ground, not oozing mud.

The people trusted God. They were not afraid. They could see the Ark in the middle of the river bed. They knew God was with them. Finally they were all safe on shore. They were in their homeland! Hundreds of years before God had promised this land to His people. (See Genesis 15:15; Exodus 15:17.) And He was faithful to His word.

3. TWO MEMORIALS SET UP
Joshua 4:1-18

Before the Israelites crossed the Jordan River, God had told Joshua to pick 12 men–one from each of the tribes–to do something special.

Joshua called the 12 tribal men. He commanded, "Go to the middle of the river where the priests are standing. Each one get a rock and bring it here."

The 12 men obeyed.

Then Joshua walked out to the priests. There he set up a pillar with 12 stones to remind them of what had happened there. On the shore at a place called Gilgal the people set up their camp. Joshua erected another pillar with the 12 rocks the men had carried out of the river.

Show Illustration #11

"Are you wondering why I am doing this?" Joshua asked. The people nodded. After what had happened that day, they had great respect for Joshua. They knew he was God's chosen leader for them just as Moses had been. They were ready to listen to him.

Joshua explained, "God commanded me to set up these memorials for two reasons. First, He does not want you ever to forget what He did for us today." Pointing to the pillars, he continued, "These stones will always be reminders that God stopped the Jordan River so we could walk across. When your children ask you why these rocks are set up here, tell them about the miracle God performed for us today."

Joshua encouraged the people saying, "No matter what happens in the days ahead, we know we can trust God. He is faithful to His word."

Everyone nodded in agreement.

"But there is another reason why God commanded me to set up these pillars. He wants the nations around us to know that He is different from the idols they worship. They will hear what God did for us today. When they see the pillars they will be reminded that our God is living and powerful. This will make them fear Him and be afraid of us," Joshua explained.

This was good news for the Israelites. They knew their enemies in Canaan were strong. But God was more powerful than any enemy they would meet. And He would not fail them.

God then told Joshua to command the priests to come up out of the Jordan. As soon as their feet touched the land, the waters came rushing back just as they were before!

How do you think you would have felt if you had been in the crowd that day? (Stimulate discussion: Awe, thanksgiving, praise, respect for God, fear of disobeying God, etc.)

4. GOD'S FAITHFULNESS TO US

Maybe you are thinking God did all that for the people of Israel, but what does that have to do with me today?

Show Illustration #12

In Hebrews 13:8 we read that He is the same today as He was long ago. Hundreds and hundreds of years ago in the time of Moses, God wrote His commands on stone tablets. And those commands have never changed. Later His Word was written on scrolls. Today the Word of God is in a book–the Bible–and everything in it is absolutely true. God cannot and will not fail us if we believe and obey His Word. God is true to His Word. (See 2 Timothy 2:13; Hebrews 6:18.) We can trust Him completely.

God still loves to do what seems impossible. (See Matthew 19:26; Mark 10:27; Luke 1:37.) The priests had to obey God and step into the river. Then God rolled back the water. When we believe God and obey Him, then He works wonders for us, too. (See John 11:40.) Would you like to share with us some present-day wonder that God has done for you? Has He supplied in a special way something you needed? Has He led you in some decision? If God has not done anything for you, is it because you have not been obedient to Him? Or have you not claimed His promises? Do you know some of His promises?

(*Teacher:* Encourage your students to memorize promises from the Word. Some suggestions: Matthew 6:33; Philippians 4:6-7, 13, 19; 2 Timothy 1:7; John 15:7; Proverbs 28:13; 1 John 1:9; 1 Corinthians 10:13. Give them opportunity in succeeding classes to quote the promises they have learned. Encourage them, too, to tell how God has kept these promises in their situations. By all means, have them list in their notebooks the promises they are expecting God to fulfill for them and in what situations.)

Lesson 4
OUR RESPONSE TO GOD'S WORD

NOTE TO THE TEACHER

The conquest of Jericho was an adventure of faith for the Israelites. From the human standpoint, God's instructions seemed ridiculous. But God's way is far above man's way. He has all-knowledge and is worthy to be trusted.

God promised victory to the Israelites if they would obey His commands exactly and fight the battle His way. The people of Israel responded by obeying Him perfectly. They relied totally on the Lord. And God proved His faithfulness. (See Hebrews 11:30.)

God commands us today to live by faith (Romans 1:17; Hebrews 10:38). This means: (1) depending entirely on God alone who is trustworthy, confident of His faithfulness; (2) having no trust in ourselves nor relying on other people.

Faith is not simply agreeing to the truths of God's Word. Our faith is real when we willingly, lovingly obey God, acknowledging Him as Lord of our lives. Without faith it is impossible to please God (Hebrews 11:6).

To help your students understand the meaning of faith, enact the object lesson which introduces the lesson. Plan ahead for a student to bring you a frail-looking seat.

Scripture to be studied: Joshua 6

The *aim* of the lesson: To show that the Word of God is true and must be believed and accepted by faith.

What your students should *know*: Faith is believing God and obeying Him.

What your students should *feel*: A desire to live by faith.

What your students should *do*: Promise God to obey Him. By faith ask God, today, to solve their problems.

Lesson outline (for the teacher's and students' notebooks):
1. Yielding to God (Joshua 5:13-6:2).
2. Obeying God's orders (Joshua 6:3-16).
3. Honoring God's rules (Joshua 6:17-19).
4. Experiencing God's victory (Joshua 6:20-21, 23-26).

The verse to be memorized:

This book of the law shall not depart out of thy mouth; but thou shalt meditate therein day and night, that thou mayest observe to do according to all that is written therein: for then thou shalt make thy way prosperous and then thou shalt have good success. (Joshua 1:8)

THE LESSON

"Will someone please bring me something to sit on?" (When it is brought, refuse to sit on it.) "Thank you. But are you certain it will hold me? Would you be willing to sit on anything like this?"

Student says: "Oh, surely!" (Student sits down.) "See? It is safe enough. Try it. You'll see."

Teacher: "I think I shall just stand, thank you."

Let me ask you a question, class. Do I have faith in _____ (mention student's name)?

Why not? (Allow response.) Because I will not trust his word. What one thing could I do to prove that I have faith in _____ (student's name)? (Allow answer.)

All right. I shall now sit on the chair. (Sit down.) I have proved I have faith in _____ (student's name). I have relied on what he said. I have sat down. And now I know he told the truth.

To have true faith in God is to believe Him and do what He says. God commanded Joshua and the Israelites to do something which seemed foolish. Did they have faith enough to trust Him and obey? Listen!

Before Joshua and the Israelites could claim the land God had promised them, the city of Jericho had to be conquered. What do you remember about Jericho? (Review from Lesson #2.) Jericho was a small city. In fact it was more like a big, overgrown fort. Its strong walls protected it from attack. And Israel did not have the kind of weapons needed to overcome the city.

1. YIELDING TO GOD
Joshua 5:13-6:2

Joshua studied the situation. The Bible does not tell us what he thought. But it could have been like this.

I wonder what would be the best way to attack Jericho. The walls are high. The gates are huge and heavy–and well guarded. The people are equipped for war. How can we conquer Jericho?

Joshua surely remembered that God had promised to defeat the enemies of the Israelites. Do you think he asked God for His help? (Encourage discussion.)

Suddenly standing before Joshua was a man with a sword in his hand.

"Who are you?" Joshua asked. "Are you on our side or the side of our enemies?"

The man answered, "I am Captain of the Lord's army."

Show Illustration #13

Immediately Joshua realized this was the Lord Himself. Listen to what the Bible says. (Read Joshua 5:14.)

What did Joshua do? (He fell on his face; he worshiped the Lord.)

What did he say? ("What are Your commands, Lord, for me, Your servant?")

Joshua yielded to God. He said, "Lord, I will obey whatever You command."

God answered, "Joshua, take off your shoes. You are on holy ground."

Off came Joshua's shoes.

Then the Lord gave him this encouraging promise: "This is My war, Joshua. I am going to win the battle against Jericho for you. Simply trust Me and do exactly as I say."

Joshua listened carefully as God explained His plan.

2. OBEYING GOD'S ORDERS
Joshua 6:3-16

Early the next morning Joshua called the people together. "Today we shall begin our attack against Jericho," he announced. "We are going to do it God's way, not ours."

Joshua continued, "Line up in this order:

Armed soldiers first. Next, seven priests with trumpets. Following the trumpeters will be the priests carrying the Ark of God. The rest of the soldiers and other people will follow the Ark."

Everyone obeyed.

Joshua continued his instructions. "Now we shall march around the city of Jericho one time. The priests will blow their trumpets. Everyone else keep quiet. Do not say one word!"

Show Illustration #14

"Ready? Forward march!" Joshua ordered.

Hearing the trumpets, the Jericho guards scurried to the top of the city wall. Wide-eyed, they watched the Israelites march around the entire city and return to their camp. "What is the matter with those people?" they wondered.

Early the next day Joshua gave the same order. Again the Israelites marched around the city without talking. All that could be heard was the blowing of the trumpets. Then they went back to camp.

Joshua gave the same order four more days–six days in a row. He gave directions only one day at a time. God was testing His people. They did not know what was going to happen. But Joshua knew. For God had told him.

Suppose you had been an Israelite soldier. What would you have thought? (Stimulate discussion.) We do not know what they talked about. But because they were much like we are, could it have been like this?

"This surely is a strange way to capture a city," said one. "What good does it do to march around Jericho?"

"I do not understand why we are doing this," said another. "But one thing I do know: God is with us."

How did he know that? (The Ark was the visible symbol of God's presence.)

"That is right," others agreed. "God is powerful. He does not do things the way we would. Just the other day God held back the Jordan River so we could cross on dry land. He knows what He is doing. All we need do is obey Joshua's orders."

Everyone agreed.

Suppose you had lived in Jericho. How would you have felt? (Give opportunity for discussion.)

The people of Jericho were frightened even before the Israelites crossed the Jordan River. (See Joshua 2:11.) Now every day they heard the tramp, tramp, tramp of thousands of feet marching around their city. They heard the trumpeters. They watched the Israelites through the windows of the houses built on the wall. Some were brave enough to crawl on top of the city wall to watch the marchers.

Perhaps at first some laughed and mocked. But they knew the God of the Israelites worked wonderful miracles for His people. As the days went on, they became worried and afraid.

Early in the morning of the seventh day, Joshua again gave orders–different ones this time. "Today we shall march around the city of Jericho seven times. At the end of the seventh time, when I give the signal, the priests will blow the trumpets and then you all shout loudly! Do you understand?"

It sounded ridiculous. But no one questioned Joshua. No one refused to obey. All had faith in God–and in Joshua, God's appointed leader.

3. HONORING GOD'S RULES
Joshua 6:17-19

Show Illustration #15

Joshua made sure that everyone understood God's orders. He began, "Remember! SHOUT!! Then rush into the city and kill everyone except Rahab and her family. Do not spare any of the others. They are evil, wicked people. Everything they do is against God."

Why were Rahab and her family to be spared? (Review Lesson 2, emphasizing that they were saved because they trusted in God.)

Joshua continued, "Save all the silver and gold and everything made of iron and brass. All these will be dedicated to the Lord and put into the treasury. But do not take anything for yourselves! You will see beautiful things you would like to have. Do not yield to temptation. Everything else must be destroyed. These are God's orders. If you disobey, everyone will suffer. Now, FORWARD MARCH!"

4. EXPERIENCING GOD'S VICTORY
Joshua 6:20-21, 23-26

Once, twice, three times, four, five, six, seven times the Israelites marched around the city that day. And, amazingly, not once did the people of Jericho shoot arrows at them or harm them in any way.

After the seventh time around the city, Joshua commanded, "SHOUT! For the Lord has given you the city!"

More than two million people shouted as loudly as they could! Then CRASH! The walls of Jericho tumbled down flat.

Show Illustration #16

The Israelites rushed into the city and with their swords completely destroyed everybody and everything. Just as God had promised, Israel won the victory!

(*Teacher:* Read Hebrews 11:30 several times slowly to your students. Let them explain what it means. The Israelites believed God when He said they would conquer Jericho. So they responded by obeying God's commands exactly.)

God says in His Word that "without faith it is impossible to please Him" (Hebrews 11:6). He wants us to obey Him just as Joshua and the Israelites did. He wants you to trust Him and depend upon Him. We all have problems. You may have troubles which seem impossible. But God is ready to help you. He has promised to hear you when you pray. When you trust Him completely, He has promised to answer your prayers according to His will.

Some people might laugh at you. They may say you are foolish for believing God and the Bible. The people of Jericho thought the Israelites were foolish. But who was wiser–the Israelites or the people of Jericho?

God commands you and me to live by faith. (See Hebrews 10:38.) He wants us (like Joshua) to obey Him perfectly, trusting Him to solve our problems. Will you ask the Lord right now, to take care of your difficulty for you?

(*Teacher:* Have students enter in their notebooks the problem or problems which face them today. Give them time to pray silently. If they have mentioned their particular difficulty to the class, have them pray aloud. Emphasize the importance of obeying God and trusting Him completely.)